Lecture on Education

The Principles of Universal Public Education, Expressed by its Historic Founder

By Horace Mann

Published by Pantianos Classics

ISBN-13: 978-1-78987-561-4

First published in 1840

Horace Mann, photographed circa 1851

Contents

Introduction

The Act, creating the Massachusetts Board of Education, was passed, April 20, 1837. In June following, the Board was organized, and its Secretary chosen. The duties of the Secretary, as expressed in the Act, are, to "collect information of the actual condition and efficiency of the Common Schools, and other means of Popular Education; and to diffuse, as widely as possible, throughout every part of the Commonwealth, information of the most approved and successful methods of arranging the studies, and conducting the education of the young, — to the end, that all children in this Commonwealth, who depend upon Common Schools for instruction, may have the best education which those schools can be made to impart."

The Board, immediately after its organization, issued an "Address to the Public," inviting the friends of education to assemble in Convention, in their respective counties, in the ensuing autumn; and the Secretary was requested to be present at those conventions, both to obtain information in regard to the condition of the schools, and to explain to the public what were supposed to be the leading motives and objects of the Legislature, in establishing the Board.

The Author of the following Lecture, having been a member of the Legislature, when the Board was established, and conversant with the general views of its projectors and advocates, (although, at that time, without the slightest idea of ever being its Secretary,) endeavored, in preparing the Lecture, to sketch a rapid outline of deficiencies to be supplied, and of objects to be pursued, in relation to our Common-School system. The Lecture was delivered before the County Conventions, held throughout the State, in the autumn of 1837; also, before the members of the Legislature, in 1838, and before other large and intelligent assemblies; and, on all or most of these occasions, a copy was requested for the press. A period of about three years having now elapsed, and, — as far as the Author or his friends have been able to ascertain, — a general coincidence of public opinion having been expressed, both as to the summary of defects to be remedied and of ends to be aimed at, the Author now deems it proper to give the Lecture a more permanent form. He is led to take this course, lest the general exposition of the views it contains, — views, which are supposed to be in harmony with those of the Legislature that established the Board, and of the original members of the Board itself, — should be hereafter misreported by inadvertence, or misrepresented by design; and also, lest the Board should be charged, in any of its plans, with a departure from its original purposes.

As a literary production, the Lecture may need some apology, on account of the almost colloquial character of its style, and its exuberance of illustration. It was foreseen, — as it actually happened, — that most of the audiences, before whom it was to be delivered, would be of a most miscellaneous character, in respect to mental cultivation and attainments. Some persons of high education, who know and feel its value, desire the same boon for all; other persons, who are illiterate, and who therefore feel the want of an education, desire to rescue their children and their friends from suffering under the same privation. Hence, auditors, widely differing in understanding, would be likely to assemble on the same occasion; and, as far as possible, something should be addressed to the train of thought and power of comprehension, belonging to each class. A common, but very expressive phrase is current amongst us, in regard to speakers who fall into the mistake of excessive profundity, or of excessive learning, in addressing a popular audience. They are said, *to shoot over the heads of their hearers.* But, where an audience contains every grade of literary character, it may be compared to a company of men scattered up and down an extensive hillside; and, if the speaker does not direct his remarks above the heads of the lowest, they will be sure to fall below the feet of the highest. This fact indicates, that he should generally aim where the collection may be supposed to be most dense, — that is, about midway between the summit and the base, — but throw an occasional shot, both above and below.

January 1, 1840

Lecture – Means and Objects of Common School Education

In pursuance of notice, contained in a circular letter, lately addressed to the school committees and friends of Education, in this county, I now appear before you, as the Secretary of the Massachusetts Board of Education. That Board was constituted by an Act of the Legislature, passed, April 20, 1837. It consists of the Governor and Lieutenant Governor of the Commonwealth, for the time being, — who are members *ex officiis,* — and of eight other gentlemen, appointed by the Executive, with the advice and consent of the Council. The object of the Board is, by extensive correspondence, by personal interviews, by the development and discussion of principles, to collect such information, on the great subject of education, as now lies scattered, buried and dormant; and after digesting, and, as far as possible, systematizing and perfecting it, to send it forth again to the extremest borders of the State, so that all improvements which are local, may be enlarged into universal; so that what is now transitory and evanescent, may be established in permanency; and that correct views, on this all-important subject, may be multiplied by the number of minds capable of understanding them.

To accomplish the object of their creation, however, the Board are clothed with no power, either restraining or directory. If they know of better modes of education, they have no authority to enforce their adoption. Nor have they any funds at their disposal. Even the services of the members are gratuitously rendered. Without authority, then, to command, and without money to remunerate or reward, their only resource, the only sinews of their strength, are, their power of appealing to an enlightened community, to rally for the promotion of its dearest interests.

Unless, therefore, the friends of Education, in different parts of the State, shall proffer their cordial and strenuous cooperation, it is obvious, that the great purposes, for which the Board was constituted, can never be accomplished. Some persons, indeed, have suggested, that the Secretary of the Board should visit the schools, individually, and impart such counsel and encouragement as he might be able; — not reflecting that such is their number and the shortness of the time during which they are kept, that, if he were to allow himself but one day for each school, to make specific examinations and to give detailed instructions, it would occupy something more than sixteen years to complete the circuit; — while the period, between the ages of four and sixteen, during which our children usually attend school, is but twelve years; so that, before the Secretary could come round upon his track again, one entire generation of scholars would have passed away, and one third of another. At his quickest speed, he would lose sight of one quarter of all the children in the State. The Board, therefore, have no voice, they have no organ, by which they can make themselves heard, in the distant villages and hamlets of this land, where those juvenile habits are now forming, where those processes of thought and feeling are, now, to-day, maturing, which, some twenty or thirty years hence, will find an arm, and become resistless might, and will uphold, or rend asunder, our social fabric. The Board may, — I trust they will, — be able to collect light and to radiate it; but upon the people, *upon the people,* will still rest the great and inspiring duty of prescribing to the next generation what their fortunes shall be, by determining in what manner they shall be educated. For it is the ancestors of a people, who prepare and predetermine all the great events in that people's history; their posterity only collect, and read them. No just judge will ever decide upon the moral responsibility of an individual, without first ascertaining what kind of parents he had; — nor will any just historian ever decide upon the honor or the infamy of a people, without placing the character of its ancestors in the judgment-balance. If the system of national instruction, devised and commenced by Charlemagne, had been continued, it would have changed the history of the French people. Such an event as the French Revolution never would have happened with free schools; any more than the American Revolution would have happened without them. The mobs, the riots, the burnings, the lynchings, perpetrated by the *men* of the present day, are perpetrated, because of their vicious or defective education, when children. We see, and feel, the havoc and the ravage of their tiger-passions, now, when they are full grown; but it was years ago that they were whelped and suckled. And so, too, if we are derelict from our duty, in this matter, our children, in their turn, will suffer. If we permit the vulture's eggs to be incubated and hatched, it will then be too late to take care of the lambs.

Some eulogize our system of Popular Education, as though worthy to be universally admired and imitated. Others pronounce it circumscribed in its action, and feeble, even where it acts. Let us waste no time in composing this strife. If good, let us improve it; if bad, let us reform it. It is of human institutions, as of men, — not any one is so good that it cannot be made better; nor so bad, that it may not become worse. Our system of education is not to be compared with those of other states or countries, merely to determine whether it may be a little more or a little less perfect than they; but it is to be contrasted with our highest ideas of perfection itself, and then the pain of the contrast to be assuaged, by improving it, forthwith and continually. The love of excellence looks ever upward towards a higher standard; it is unimproving pride and arrogance only, that are satisfied with being superior to a lower. No community should rest contented with being superior to other communities, while it is inferior to its own capabilities. And such are the beneficent ordinations of Providence, that the very thought of improving is the germination of improvement.

The science and the art of Education, like every thing human, depend upon culture, for advancement. And they would be more cultivated, if the rewards for attention, and the penalties for neglect, were better understood. When effects follow causes, — quick as thunder, lightning, — even infants and idiots learn to beware; or they act, to enjoy. They have a glimmer of reason, sufficient, in such cases, for admonition, or impulse. Now, in this world, the entire succession of events, which fills time and makes up life, is nothing but causes and effects. These causes and effects are bound and linked together by an adamantine law. And the Deity has given us power over the effects, by giving us power over the causes. This power consists in a Knowledge of the connection established between causes and effects, — enabling us to foresee the future consequences of present conduct. If you show to me a handful of perfect seeds, I *know,* that, with appropriate culture, those seeds will produce a growth after their kind; whether it be of pulse, which is ripened for human use in a month, or of oaks, whose lifetime is centuries. So, in some of the actions of men, consequences follow conduct with a lock-step; in others, the effects of youthful actions first burst forth as from a subterranean current, in advanced life. In those great relations which subsist between different generations, — between ancestors and posterity, — effects are usually separated from their causes, by long intervals of time. The pulsations of a nation's heart are to be counted, not by seconds, but by years. Now, it is in this class of cases, where there are long intervals lying between our conduct and its consequences; where one generation sows, and another generation reaps; — it is in this class of cases, that the greatest and most sorrowful of human errors originate. Yet, even for these, a benevolent Creator has supplied us with an antidote. He has given us the faculty of reason, whose especial office and function it is, to discover the connection between causes and effects; and thereby to enable us so to regulate the causes of to-day, as to predestinate the effects of to-morrow. In the eye of reason, causes and effects exist in proximity, — in juxtaposition. They lie side by side, whatever length of time, or distance of space, comes in between them. If I am guilty of an act or a neglect, to-day, which will certainly cause the infliction of a wrong, it matters not whether that wrong happen, on the other side of the globe, or in the next century. Whenever or wherever it happens, it is mine; it belongs to me; my conscience owns it; and no sophistry can give me absolution. Who would think of acquitting an incendiary, because the train which he had laid and lighted, first circuited the globe before it reached and consumed his neighbor's dwelling? From the nature of the case, in education, the effects are widely separated from the causes. They happen so long afterwards, that the reason of the community loses sight of the connection between them. It does not bring the cause and the effect together, and lay them, and look at them, side by side.

If, instead of twenty-one *years,* the course of Nature allowed but twenty-one *days,* to rear an infant to the full stature of manhood, and to sow in his bosom, the seeds of unbounded happiness or of unspeakable misery, — I suppose, in that case, the merchant would abandon his bargains, and the farmer would leave the ingathering of his harvests, and even the drunkard would hie homeward from the midst of his revel, and *that* twenty-one days would be spent, without much sleep, and with many prayers. And yet, it cannot be denied, that the consequences of a vicious education, inflicted upon a child, are now precisely the same as they would be, if, at the end of twenty-one days after an infant's birth, his tongue were already roughened with oaths and blasphemy; or he were seen skulking through society, obtaining credit upon false pretences, or with rolls of counterfeit bills in his pocket; or were already expiating his offences in the bondage and infamy of a prison. And the consequences of a virtuous education, at the end of twenty-one years, are now precisely the same as they would be, if, at the end of twenty-one days after his birth, the infant had risen from his cradle into the majestic form of manhood, and were possessed of all those qualities and attributes, which a being created in the image of God ought to have; — with a power of fifty years of beneficent labor compacted into his frame; — with nerves of sympathy, reaching out from his own heart and twining around the heart of society, so that the great social wants of men should be a part of his consciousness;— and with a mind able to perceive what is right, prompt to defend it, or, if need be, to die for it. It ought to be understood, that none of these consequences become any the less certain, because they are more remote. It ought to be universally understood and intimately felt, that, in regard to children, all precept and example;

all kindness and harshness; all rebuke and commendation; all forms, indeed, of direct or indirect education; affect mental growth, just as dew, and sun, and shower, or untimely frost, affect vegetable growth. Their influences are integrated and made one with the soul. They enter into spiritual combination with it, never afterwards to be wholly decompounded. They are like the daily food eaten by wild game, — so pungent and saporific in its nature, that it flavors every fibre of their flesh, and colors every bone in their body. Indeed, so pervading and enduring is the effect of education upon the youthful soul, that it may well be compared to a certain species of writing-ink, whose color, at first, is scarcely perceptible, but which penetrates deeper and grows blacker by age, until, if you consume the scroll over a coal-fire, the character will still be legible in the cinders. It ought to be understood and felt, that, however it may be, in a social or jurisprudential sense, it is nevertheless true, in the most solemn and dread-inspiring sense, that, by an irrepealable law of Nature, the iniquities of the fathers are still visited upon the children, unto the third and fourth generation. Nor do the children suffer for the iniquities only, of their parents; they suffer for their neglect and even for their ignorance. Hence, I have always admired that law of the Icelanders, by which, when a minor child commits an offence, the courts first make judicial inquiry, whether his parents have given him a good education; and, if it be proved they have not, the child is acquitted and the parents are punished. In both the old Colonies of Plymouth, and of Massachusetts Bay, if a child, over sixteen, and under twenty-one years of age, committed a certain capital offence against father or mother, he was allowed to arrest judgment of death upon himself, by showing that his parents, in the language of the law, "had been very unchristianly negligent in his education."

How, then, are the purposes of education to be accomplished? However other worlds may be, this world of ours is evidently constructed on the plan of producing ends by using means. Even the Deity, with his Omniscience and his Omnipotence, carries forward our system, by processes so minute, and movements so subtile, as generally to elude our keenest inspection. He might speak all the harvests of the earth, and all the races of animals and of men into full-formed existence, at a word; and yet, the tree is elaborated from the kernel, and the wing from the chrysalis, by a series of processes, which occupies years, and sometimes centuries, for its completion. Education, more than any thing else, demands not only a scientific acquaintance with mental laws, but the nicest art in the detail and the application of means, for its successful prosecution; because influences, imperceptible in childhood, work out more and more broadly into beauty or deformity, in afterlife. No unskilful hand should ever play upon a harp, where the tones are left, forever, in the strings.

In the first place, the best methods should be well ascertained; in the second, they should be universally diffused. In this Commonwealth; there are about three thousand Public Schools, in all of which the rudiments of knowledge are taught. These schools, at the present time, are so many distinct, independent communities; each being governed by its own habits, traditions, and local customs. There is no common, superintending power over them; there is no bond of brotherhood or family between them. They are strangers and aliens to each other. The teachers are, as it were, imbedded, each in his own school district; and they are yet to be excavated, and brought together, and to be established, each as a polished pillar of a holy temple. As the system is now administered, if any improvement in principles or modes of teaching is discovered by talent or accident, in one school,— instead of being published to the world, it dies with the discoverer. No means exist for multiplying new truths, or even for preserving old ones. A gentleman, filling one of the highest civil offices in this Commonwealth, — a resident in one of the oldest counties and in one of the largest towns in the State, — a sincere friend of the cause of education, — recently put into my hands a printed report, drawn up by a clergyman of much repute, which described, as was supposed, an important improvement, in relation to our Common Schools, and earnestly enjoined its general adoption; when it happened to be within my own knowledge, that the supposed new discovery had been in successful operation for sixteen years, in a town but little more than sixteen miles distant. Now, in other things, we act otherwise. If a manufacturer discover a new combination of wheels, or a new mode of applying water or steam-power, by which stock can be economized, or the value of fabrics enhanced ten per cent., the information flies over the country, at once; the old machinery is discarded, the new is substituted. Nay, it is difficult for an inventor to preserve the secret of his invention, until he can secure it by letters-patent. Our mechanics seem to possess a sort of keen, greyhound faculty, by which they can scent an improvement afar off. They will sometimes go, in disguise, to the inventor and offer themselves as workmen; and instances have been known of their breaking into his workshop, by night, and purloining the invention. And hence that progress in the mechanic arts, which has given a name to the age in which we live, and made it a common wonder. Improvements in useful, and often in useless, arts, command solid prices, — twenty, fifty, or even a hundred, thousand dollars, — while improvements in education, in the means of obtaining new guaranties, for the permanence of all we hold dear, and for making our children and our children's children wiser and happier, — these are scarcely topics of conversation or inquiry. Do we not need, then, some new and living institution, some animate organization, which shall at least embody and diffuse all that is now known on this subject, and thereby save, every year, hundreds of children from being sacrificed to experiments which have been a hundred times exploded?

Before noticing some particulars, in which a common channel for receiving and for disseminating information, may subserve the prosperity of our Common Schools, allow me to praise, that there is one rule, which, in all places and in all forms of education, should be held as primary, paramount, and, as far as possible, exclusive. Acquirement and pleasure should go hand in hand. They should never part company. The pleasure of acquiring should be the incitement to acquire. A child is wholly incapable of appreciating the ultimate value or uses of knowledge. In its early beginnings, the motive of general, future utility will be urged in vain. Tell an abecedarian, as an inducement to learn his letters, of the sublimities of poetry and eloquence, that may be wrought out of the alphabet; and to him it is not so good as moonshine. Let me ask any man, whether he ever had, when a child, any just conception of the uses, to which he is now, as a man, daily applying his knowledge. How vain is it, then, to urge upon a child, as a motive to study, that which he cannot possibly understand! Nor is the motive of fear preferable. Fear is one of the most debasing and dementalizing of all the passions. The sentiment of fear was given us, that it might be roused into action, by whatever should be shunned, scorned, abhorred. The emotion should never be associated with what is to be desired, toiled for, and loved. If a child appetizes his books, then, lesson-getting is free labor. If he revolts at them, then, it is slave-labor. Less is done, and the little is not so well done. Nature has implanted a feeling of curiosity in the breast of every child, as if to make herself certain of his activity and progress. The desire of learning alternates with the desire of food; the mental with the bodily appetite. The former is even more craving and exigent, in its nature, than the latter, and acts longer without satiety. Men sit with folded arms, even while they are surrounded by objects of which they know nothing. Who ever saw that done by a child? But we cloy, disgust, half-extirpate, this appetite for knowledge, and then deny its existence. Mark a child, when a clear, well-defined, vivid conception seizes it. The whole nervous tissue vibrates; every muscle leaps; every joint plays. The face becomes auroral. The spirit flashes through the body, like lightning through a cloud. Tell a child the simplest story, which is adapted to his present state of mental advancement, and therefore intelligible — and he will forget sleep, leave food untasted, nor would he be enticed from hearing it, though you gave him, for playthings, shining fragments broken off from the sun. Observe the blind, and the deaf and dumb. So strong is their inborn desire for knowledge, that, although those natural inlets, the eye and the ear, are closed; yet, such are the amazing attractive forces of the mind for it, that they will draw it inward, through the solid walls and encasements of the body. If the eye be curtained with darkness, it will enter through the ear. If the ear be closed in silence, it will ascend along the nerves of touch. Every new idea, that enters in the presence of the sovereign mind, carries offerings of delight with it, to make its coming welcome. Indeed, our Maker created us in blank ignorance for the very purpose of giving us the boundless, endless pleasure of learning new things; and the true path for the human intellect leads from ignorance to omniscience, — ascending by an infinity of truths, each novel and delightful.

The voice of Nature, therefore, forbids the infliction of annoyance, discomfort, pain, upon a child, while engaged in study. If he actually suffers from position, or heat, or cold, or fear, not only is a portion of the energy of his mind withdrawn from his lesson, — all of which should be concentrated upon it; but, at that undiscriminating age, the pain blends itself with the study, makes part of the remembrance of it, and thus curiosity and the love of learning are deadened, or turned away towards vicious objects. This is the philosophy of children's hating study. We insulate them by fear; we touch them with nonconductors; and then, because they emit no spark, we gravely aver that they are non-electric bodies. If possible, pleasure should be made to flow like a sweet atmosphere around the early learner, and pain be kept beyond the association of ideas. You cannot open blossoms with a northeast storm. The buds of the hardiest plants will wait for the genial influences of the sun, though they perish, while waiting.

The first practical application of these truths, in relation to our Common Schools, is to Schoolhouse Architecture, — a subject so little regarded, yet so vitally important. The construction of schoolhouses involves, not the love of study and proficiency, only, but health and length of life. 1 have the testimony of many eminent physicians to this fact. They assure me that it is within their own personal knowledge, that there is, annually, loss of life, destruction of health, and such anatomical distortion as renders life hardly worth possessing, growing out of the bad construction of our schoolhouses. Nor is this evil confined to a few of them, only. It is a very general calamity. I have seen many schoolhouses, in central districts of rich and populous towns, where each seat connected with a desk, consisted only of an upright post or pedestal, jutting up out of the floor, the upper end of which was only about eight or ten inches square, without side-arms or backboard; and some of them so high that the feet of the children in vain sought after the floor. They were beyond soundings. Yet, on the hard top of these stumps, the masters and misses of the school must balance themselves, as well as they can, for six hours in a day. All attempts to preserve silence in such a house are not only vain, but cruel. Nothing but absolute empalement could keep a live child still, on such a seat; and you would hardly think him worth living, if it could. The pupils will resort to every possible bodily evolution for relief; and, after all, though they may *change the place, they keep the pain*. I have good reasons for remembering one of another class of schoolhouses, which the scientific would probably call the *sixth* order of architecture, — the wicker-work order, summer-houses for winter residence, — where there never was a severely cold day, without the ink's freezing in the pens of the scholars while they were writing; and the teacher was literally obliged to compromise between the sufferings of those who were exposed to the cold of the windows and those exposed to the heat of the fire, by not raising the thermometer of the latter above ninety degrees, until that of the former fell below thirty. A part of the children suffered the Arctic cold of Captains Ross and Parry, and a part, the torrid heat of the Landers, without, in either case, winning the honors of a discoverer. It was an excellent place for the teacher to illustrate one of the facts in geography; for five steps would have carried him through the five zones. Just before my present circuit, I passed a schoolhouse, the roof of which, on one side, was trough-like; and down towards the eaves there was a large hole; so that the whole operated like a tunnel to catch all the rain and pour it into the schoolroom. At first, I did not know but it might be some apparatus designed to explain the Deluge. I called and inquired of the mistress, if she and her little ones were not sometimes drowned out. She said she should be, only that the floor leaked as badly as the roof, and drained off the water. And yet a healthful, comfortable schoolhouse can be erected as cheaply as one, which, judging from its construction, you would say, had been dedicated to the evil genius of deformity and suffering.

There is another evil in the construction of our schoolhouses, whose immediate consequences are not so bad, though their remote ones are indefinitely worse. No fact is now better established than that a man cannot live, without a supply of about a gallon of fresh air, every minute; nor enjoy good health, indeed, without much more. The common air, as is now well known, is mainly composed of two ingredients, one only of which can sustain life. The action of the lungs upon the vital portion of the air, changes its very nature, converting it from a life-sustaining to a life-destroying element. As we inhale a portion of the atmosphere, it is healthful; — the same portion, as we exhale it, is poisonous. Hence, ventilation in rooms, especially where large numbers are collected, is a condition of health and life. Privation admits of no excuse. To deprive a child of comfortable clothes, or wholesome food, or fuel, may sometimes, possibly, be palliated. These cost money, and often draw hardly upon the scanty resources of the poor. But what shall we say of stinting and starving a child, in regard to this prime necessary of life? — of holding his mouth, as it were, lest he should obtain a sufficiency of that vital element, which God, in His munificence, has poured out, a hundred miles deep, all around the globe? Of productions, reared or transported by human toil, there may be a dearth. At any rate, frugality in such things is commendable. But to put a child on short allowances out of this sky-full of air, is enough to make a miser weep. It is as absurd, as it would have been for Noah, while the torrents of rain were still descending, to have put his family upon short allowances of water. This vast quantity of air was given us to supersede the necessity of ever using it at second-hand. Heaven has ordained this matter with adorable wisdom. That very portion of the air which we turn into poison, by respiring it, becomes the aliment of vegetation. What is death to us, is life to all verdure and flowerage. And again, vegetation rejects the ingredient which is life to us. Thus the equilibrium is forever restored; or rather, it is never destroyed. In this perpetual circuit, the atmosphere is forever renovated, and made the sustainer of life, both for the animal and vegetable worlds.

A simple contrivance for ventilating the schoolroom, unattended with any perceptible expense, would rescue children from this fatal, though unseen evil. It is an indisputable fact, that, for years past, far more attention has been paid, in this respect, to the construction of jails and prisons, than to that of schoolhouses. Yet, why should we treat our felons better than our children? I have observed in all our cities and populous towns, that, wherever stables have been recently built, provision has been made for their ventilation. This is encouraging, for I hope the children's turn will come, when gentlemen shall have taken care of their horses. I implore physicians to act upon this evil. Let it be removed, extirpated, cut off, surgically.

I cannot here stop to give even an index of the advantages of an agreeable site for a schoolhouse; of attractive, external appearance; of internal finish, neatness, and adaptation; nor of the still more important subject of having two rooms for all large schools, — both on the same floor, or one over the other, — so as to allow a separation of the large from the small scholars, for the purpose of placing the latter, at least, under the care of a female teacher. Each of these topics, and especially the last, is worthy of a separate essay. Allow me, however, to remark, in passing, that I regard it as one of the clearest ordinances of nature, that woman is the appointed guide and guardian of children of a tender age. And she does not forego, but, in the eye of prophetic vision, she anticipates and makes her own, all the immortal honors of the academy, the forum, and the senate, when she lays their deep foundations, by training up children in the way they should so.

A great mischief, — I use the word *mischief,* because it implies a certain degree of wickedness, — a great mischief is suffered in the diversity and multiplicity of our school books. Not more than twenty or thirty different kinds of books, exclusive of a school library, are needed in our Common Schools; and yet, though I should not dare state the fact, if I had not personally sought out the information from most authentic sources, there are now, in actual use in the schools of this State, more than three hundred different kinds of books; and, in the markets of this and the neighboring States, seeking for our adoption, I know not how many hundreds more. The standards, in spelling, pronunciation, and writing; in rules of grammar and in processes in arithmetic, are as various as the books. Correct language, in one place, is provincialism in another. While we agree in regarding the confusion of Babel as a judgment, we unite in confounding it more, as though it were a blessing. But is not uniformity on these subjects desirable? Are there not some of these books, to which all good judges, on comparison, would award the preference? Could they not be afforded much cheaper for the great market which uniformity would open; thus furnishing better books at lower prices? And why not teach children aright, the first time? It is much harder to unlearn than to learn. Why go through three processes instead of one, by first learning, then unlearning, and then learning, again? This mischief grew out of the immense profits formerly realized from the manufacture of school books. There seems never to have been any difficulty in procuring reams of recommendations, because patrons have acted under no responsibility. An edition once published must be sold; for the date has become almost as important in school books, as in almanacs. All manner of devices are daily used to displace the old books, and to foist in new ones. The compiler has a cousin in the town of A, who will decry the old and recommend the new; or a literary gentleman in the city of B has just published some book on a different subject, and is willing to exchange recommendations, eyen; or the author has a mechanical friend, in a neighboring town, who has just patented some new tool, and who will recommend the author's book, if the author will recommend his tool. Publishers often employ agents to hawk their books about the country; and I have known several instances where such a pedlar, — or picaroon, — has taken all the old books of a whole class in school, in exchange for his new ones, book for book, — looking, of course, to his chance of making sales after the book bad been established in the school, for reimbursement and profits; so that at last, the children have to pay for what they supposed was given them. On this subject, too, cannot the mature views of competent and disinterested men, residing, respectively, in all parts of the State, be the means of effecting a much-needed reform?

There is another point, where, as it seems to me, a united effort among the friends of education would, in certain branches of instruction, increase tenfold the efficiency of our Common Schools. I mean, the use of some simple apparatus, so as to employ the eye, more than the ear, in the acquisition of knowledge. After the earliest years of childhood, the superiority of the eye over the other senses, in quickness, in precision, in the vastness of its field of operations, and in its power of penetrating, like a flash, into any interstices, where light can go and come, is almost infinite. The senses of taste, and smell, and touch, seem to be more the servants of the body than of the soul; and, amongst the infinite variety of objects in the external world, hearing takes notice of sounds only. Close your eyes, and then, with the aid of the other senses, examine a watch, an artisan's workshop, a manufactory, a ship, a steam-engine; and how meagre and formless are all the ideas they present to you. But the eye is the great thoroughfare between the outward and material infinite, and the inward and spiritual infinite. The mind often acquires, by a glance of the eye, what volumes of books and months of study could not reveal so livingly through the ear. Every thing that comes through the eye, too, has a vividness, a clear outline, a just collocation of parts, — each in its proper place, — which the other senses can never communicate. Ideas or impressions acquired through vision are long-lived. Those acquired through the agency of the other senses often die young. Hence, the immeasurable superiority of this organ is founded in Nature. There is a fund of truth in the old saying, that "seeing is believing." There never will be any such maxim, in regard to the other senses. To use the ear instead of the eye, in any case where the latter is available, is as preposterous, as it would be for our migratory birds, in their overland passage, to walk rather than to fly. We laugh at the Germans, because in using their oxen, they attach the load to the horns, instead of the neck; but do we not commit a much greater absurdity, in communicating knowledge through the narrow fissure of the ear, which holds communication only with a small circle of things, and in that circle, only with things that utter a sound, instead of conveying it through the broad portals of the earth and heaven surveying eye. Nine tenths, — may I not say ninety-nine hundredths, — of all our Common School instruction are conveyed through the ear; or, — which is the same thing, — through the medium of written instead of spoken words, where the eye has been taught to do the work of the ear. In teaching those parts of geography which comprise the outlines and natural features of the earth, and in astronomy, the use of the globe and the planetarium would reduce the labor of months to as many hours. Ocular evidence, also, is often indispensable for correcting the imperfections of language, as it is understood by a child. For instance, (and I take this illustration from fact and not from imagination,) a child, born in the interior, and who has never seen the ocean, is taught that the earth is *surrounded* by an elastic medium, called the atmosphere. He thereby gets the idea of perfect circumfusion and envelopment. In the next lesson, he is taught that an island is a small body of land *surrounded* by water. If he has a quick mind, he may get the idea that an island is land, enveloped in water, as the earth is in air. Mature minds always modify the meaning of words and sentences by numerous rules, of which a child knows nothing. If, when speaking of the Deity to a man of common intelligence, I use the word "power," he understands omnipotence; and if I use the same word when speaking of an ant, he understands that I mean strength enough to lift a grain; — but a child would require explanations, limiting the meaning of the word in the one case, and extending it in the other.

Other things being equal, the pleasure which a child enjoys, in studying or contemplating, is proportioned to the liveliness of his perceptions and ideas. A child who spurns books, will be attracted and delighted by visible objects of well-defined forms and striking colors. In the one case, he things through a haze; in the other, by sunlight A contemplative child, whose mind gets as vivid images from reading as from gazing, always prefers reading. Although it is undoubtedly true, that taste and predilection, in regard to any subject, will give brightness and distinctness to ideas; yet it is also true that bright and distinct ideas will greatly modify tastes and predilections. Now the eye may be employed much more extensively than it ever has been, in giving what I will venture to call the geography of ideas, that is, a perception, where one idea bounds on another, — where the province of one idea ends, and that of the adjacent ideas begins. Could children be habituated to fixing these lines of demarcation, to seeing and feeling ideas as distinctly as though they were geometrical solids, they would then experience an insupportable uneasiness, whenever they were lost in fog-land and among the Isles of the Mist; and this uneasiness would enforce investigation, survey, and perpetual outlook; and in afterlife, a power would exist of applying luminous and exact thought to extensive combinations of facts and principles, and we should have the materials of philosophers, statesmen and chief-justices. The pleasure which children enjoy in visiting our miserable toy-shop collections, — the dreams of crazy brains, *done* into wood and pewter, — comes mainly from the vividness, the oneness, wholeness, completeness, of their perceptions. The gewgaws do not give delight, because of their grotesqueness, but in spite of it. Natural ideas derived through a microscope, or from any mechanism which would stamp as deep an imprint and glow with as quick a vitality, would give them far greater delight. And how different, as to attainments in useful knowledge, would children be, at the end of eight or ten years. accordingly as they had sought their gratification, from one or the other of these sources.

And what higher delight, what reward, at once so innocent and so elevating, as to explain by means of suitable apparatus, to the larger scholars in a school, the cause and manner of an eclipse of the sun or moon! And when those impressive phenomena occur, how beautiful to witness the manifestations of wonder and of reverence for God, which spring spontaneously from the intelligent observation of such sublime spectacles; instead of their being regarded with the horrible imaginings of superstition, or with such stupid amazement, as belongs only to the brutes that perish! If a model were given, every ingenious boy, with a few broken window panes and a pocket-knife, could make a prism. With this, the rainbow, the changing colors of the dew-drop, the gorgeous light of the sunset sky, could be explained; and thus might the minds of children be early imbued with a love of pure and beautiful things, and led upward towards the angel, instead of downward towards the brute, from this middle ground of humanity. Imbue the young mind with these sacred influences, and they will forever constitute a part of its moral being; they will abide with it and tend to uphold and purify it, wherever it may be cast by fortune, in this tumultuous arena of life. A spirit so softened and penetrated, will be,

> "Like the vase in which roses hare once been distill'd;
> You may break, you may ruin the vase, if you will,
> But the scent of the roses will hang round it still."

At the last session of the Legislature, a law was enacted, authorizing school districts to raise money for the purchase of apparatus and Common School libraries, for the use of the children, to be expended in sums not exceeding thirty dollars, for the first year, and ten dollars, for any succeeding year. Trifling as this may appear, yet I regard the law as hardly second in importance to any which has been passed since the year 1647, when Common Schools were established. Every district can find some secure place for preserving them, until, in repairing or rebuilding schoolhouses, a separate apartment can be provided for their safe-keeping. As soon as one half the benefits of these instruments of learning shall be understood, I doubt not that public-spirited individuals will be found, in most towns, who will contribute something to the library; and artisans, too, who will feel an honorable pleasure in adding something to the apparatus, wrought by their own hands, — perhaps devised by their own ingenuity. "Build dove-holes," says the proverb, "and the doves will come." And what purer satisfaction, what more sacred object of ambition, can any man propose to himself, than to give the first impulse to an improvement, which will go on increasing in value, forever! It may be said, that mischievous children will destroy or mutilate whatever is obtained for this purpose. But children will not destroy or injure what gives them pleasure. Indeed, the love of malicious mischief, the proneness to deface whatever is beautiful, — this vile ingredient in the old Saxon blood, wherever it flows, — originated, and it is aggravated, by the almost total want, amongst us, of objects of beauty, taste, and elegance, for our children to grow up with, to admire, and to protect.

The expediency of having District School Libraries is fast becoming a necessity. It is too late to stop the art of printing, or to arrest the general circulation of books. Reading of some kind, the children will have; and the question is, whether it is best, that this reading should be supplied to them by the choice of men, whose sole object is gain; or whether it shall be prepared by wise and benevolent men, whose object is to do good. Probably, not one child in ten, in this State, has free access to any library of useful and entertaining knowledge. Where there are town, parish, or social libraries, they either do not consist of suitable books, or they are burdened with restrictions which exclude more than are admitted. A District School Library would be open to all the children in the district. They would enter it independently. Wherever there is genius, the library would nourish it. Talents would not die of inaction, for want of some sphere for exercise. Habits of reading and reflection would be formed, instead of habits of idleness and malicious mischief. The wealth and prosperity of Massachusetts are not owing to natural position or resources. They exist, in despite of a sterile soil and an inhospitable clime. They do not come from the earth, but from the ingenuity and frugality of the people. Their origin is good thinking, carried out into good action; and intelligent reading in a child will result in good thinking in the man or woman. But there is danger, it is said, of reading bad books. So there is danger of eating bad food; shall we therefore have no harvests? No! It was the kindling excitement of a few books, by which those Massachusetts boys, John Adams and Benjamin Franklin, first struck out an intellectual spark, which broadened into magnitude and brightened into splendor, until it became a mighty luminary, which now stands, and shall forever stand, among the greater lights in the firmament of glory.

But in the selection of books for school libraries, let every man stand upon his honor, and never ask for the introduction of any book, because it favors the distinctive views of his sect or party. A wise man prizes only the free and intelligent assent of unprejudiced minds; he disdains a slavish and non-compos echo, even to his best-loved opinions. In striving together for a common end, peculiar ends must neither be advocated nor assailed. Strengthen the intellect of children, by exercise upon the objects and laws of Nature; train their feelings to habits of order, industry, temperance, justice; to the love of man, because of his wants, and to the love of God, because of his universally acknowledged perfections; and, so far as public measures, applicable to all, can reach, you have the highest human assurance, that, when they grow up, they will adopt your favorite opinions, if they are right, or discover the true reasons for discarding them, if they are wrong.

An advantage altogether invaluable, of supplying a child, by means of a library and of apparatus, with vivid ideas and illustrations, is, that he may always be possessed, in his own mind, of correct standards and types with which to compare whatever objects he may see in his excursions abroad; — and that he may also have useful subjects of reflection, whenever his attention is not engrossed by external things. A boy who is made clearly to understand the philosophical principle on which he flies his kite, and then to recognize the same principle in a wind or a water-wheel, and in the sailing of a ship; — wherever business or pleasure may afterwards lead him, if he sees that principle in operation, he will mentally refer to it, and think out its applications, when, otherwise, he would be singing or whistling. Twenty years would work out immense results from such daily observation and reflection. Dr. Franklin attributed much of his practical turn of mind, — which was the salient point of his immortality, — to the fact, that his father, in his conversations before the family, always discussed some useful subject, or developed some just principle of individual or social action, instead of talking forever about trout-catching or grouse-shooting; about dogs, dinners, dice, or trumps. In its moral bearings this subject grows into immense importance. How many months, — may I not say years, — in a child's life, when, with spontaneous activity, his mind hovers and floats wherever it listeth! As he sits at home, amid familiar objects, or walks frequented paths, or lies listlessly in his bed, if his mind be not preoccupied with some substantial subjects of thought, the best that you can hope is, that it will wander through dream-land, and expend its activity in chasing shadows. Far more probable is it, especially if the child is exposed to the contamination of profane or obscene minds, that in these seasons of solitude and reverie, the cockatrice's eggs of impure thoughts and desires will be hatched. And what *boy,* at least, is there who is not in daily peril of being corrupted by the evil communications of his elders? We all know, that there are self-styled gentlemen amongst us, — *self-styled gentlemen,* — who daily, and hourly, lap their tongues in the foulness of profanity; and though, through a morally-insane perversion, they may restrain themselves, in the presence of ladies and of clergymen, yet it is only for the passing hour, when they hesitate not to pour out the pent-up flood, to deluge and defile the spotless purity of childhood, — and this, too, at an age, when these polluting stains sink, centre-deep, into their young and tender hearts, so that no moral bleachery can ever afterwards wholly cleanse and purify them. No parent, no teacher, can ever feel any rational security about the growth of the moral nature of his child, unless he contrives in some way to learn the tenor of his secret, silent meditations, or prepares the means, beforehand, of determining what those meditations shall be. A child may soon find it no difficult thing, to universe and act by a set of approved rules, and then to retire into the secret chambers of his own soul, and there to riot and gloat upon guilty pleasures, whose act would be perdition, and would turn the fondest home into a hell. But there is an antidote, — I do not say for all, but for most, of this peril. The mind of children can be supplied with vivid illustrations of the works of Nature and of Art; its chambers can be hung round with picture-thoughts and images of truth, and charity, and justice, and affection, which will be companions to the soul, when no earthly friend can accompany it.

It is only a further development of this topic, to consider the inaptitude of many of our educational processes, for making accurately-thinking minds. It has been said by some one, that the good sense and sound judgment, which we find in the community, are only what have escaped the general ravage of a bad education. School studies ought to be so arranged, as to promote a harmonious development of the faculties. In despotic Prussia, a special science is cultivated, under the name of *methodik,* the scope of which is to arrange and adapt studies, so as to meet the wants and exercise the powers of the opening mind. In free America, we have not the name; indeed, we can scarcely be said to have the idea. Surely, the farmer, the gardener, the florist, who have established rules for cultivating every species of grain, and fruit, and flower, cannot doubt, that, in the unfolding and expanding of the young mini, some processes will be congenial, others fatal. Those whose business it is to compound ingredients, in any art, weigh them with the nicest exactness, and watch the precise moments of their chemical combinations. The mechanic selects all his materials with the nicest care, and measures all their dimensions to a hair's breadth; and he knows that if he fails in aught, he will produce a weak, loose, irregular fabric. Indeed, can you name any business, avocation, profession, or employment, whatever, — even to the making of hobnails or wooden skewers, — where chance, ignorance, or accident, is ever rewarded with a perfect product? But in no calling is there such a diversity as in education, — diversity in principles, diversity in the application of those principles. Discussion, elucidation, the light of a thousand minds brought to a focus, would result in discarding the worst and in improving even the best. Under this head are included the great questions respecting the order and succession of studies; the periods of alternation between them; the proportion between the exact and the approximate sciences; and what is principal and what is subsidiary, in pursuing them.

There is a natural order and progression in the development of the faculties: "First the blade, then the ear, afterwards the full corn in the ear." And in the mind, as in the grain, the blade may be so treated that the full corn will never appear. For instance, if any faculty is brooded upon and warmed into life before the period of its natural development, it will have a precocious growth, to be followed by weakness, or by a want of symmetry and proportion in the whole character. Consequences still worse will follow, where faculties are cultivated in the reverse order of their natural development. Again, if collective ideas are forced into a child's mind, without his being made to analyze them, and understand the individual ideas of which they are composed, the probability is, that the collective idea will never be comprehended. Let me illustrate this position by a case where it is least likely to happen, that we may form some idea of its frequency in other things. A child is taught to count *ten*. He is taught to repeat the words, *one, two,* &c., as words, merely; and if care be not taken, he will attach no more comprehensive idea to the word *ten,* than he did to the word *one.* He will not think of ten ones, as he uses it. In the same way, he proceeds to use the words, hundred, thousand, million, &c., — the idea in his mind, not keeping within hailing distance of the signification of the words used. Hence there is generated a habit of using words, not as the representatives of ideas, but as sounds, merely. How few children there are of the age of sixteen years, — an age at which almost all of them have ceased to attend upon our schools, — who have any adequate conception of the power of the signs they have been using. How few of them know even so simple a truth as this, that, if they were to count one, every second, for ten hours in a day, without intermission, it would take about twenty-eight days to count a million. Yet they have been talking of millions, and hundreds of millions, as though they were units. Now, suppose you speak to such a person of millions of children, growing up under a highly elaborated system of vicious education, unbalanced by any good influences; or suppose you appeal to him, in behalf of a million of people wailing beneath the smitings of the oppressor's rod, — he gets no distinct idea of so many as fifty; and therefore he has no intellectual substratum, upon which to found an appropriate feeling, or by which to graduate its intensity.

Again; in geography, we put a quarto-sized map, or perhaps a globe no larger than a goose's egg, into a child's hands, and we invite him to spread out his mind over continents, oceans, and archipelagoes, at once. This process does not expand the mind of the child to the dimensions of the objects, but it belittles the objects to the nutshell capacity of the mind. Such a course of instruction may make precocious, green-house children; but you will invariably find, that, when boys are prematurely turned into little men, they remain little men, always. Physical geography should be commenced by making a child describe and plot a room with its fixtures, a house with its apartments, the adjoining yards, fields, roads or streets, hills, waters, &c. Then embracing, if possible, the occasion of a visit to a neighboring town, or county, that should be included. Here, perpetual reference must be had to the points of the compass. After a just extension has been given to his ideas of a county, or a state, then that county or state should be shown to him on a globe; and, cost what labor or time it may, his mind must be expanded to a comprehension of relative magnitudes, so that his idea of the earth shall be as adequate to the size of the earth, as his idea of the house or the field was to the size of the house or the field. Thus the pupil founds his knowledge of unseen things upon the distinct notions of eyesight, in regard to familiar objects. Yet I believe it is not very uncommon to give the mind of the young learner a continent, for a single intellectual meal, and an ocean to wash it down with. It recently happened, in a school within my own knowledge, that a class of small scholars in geography, on being examined respecting the natural divisions of the earth, — its continents, oceans, islands, gulfs, &c., — answered all the questions with admirable precision and promptness. They were then asked, by a visitor, some general questions respecting their lesson, and, amongst others, whether they had ever seen the earth about which they had been reciting; and they unanimously declared, in good faith, that they never had. Do we not find here an explanation, why there are so many men whose conceptions on all subjects are laid down on so small a scale of miles, — so many thousand leagues to a hair's breadth? By such absurd processes, no vivid ideas can be gained, and therefore no pleasure is enjoyed. A capacity of wonder is destroyed in a day, sufficient to keep alive the flame of curiosity for years. The subjects of the lessons cease to be new, and yet are not understood. Curiosity, which is the hunger and thirst of the mind, is forever cheated and balked; for nothing but a real idea can give real, true, intellectual gratification. A habit, too, is inevitably formed of reciting, without thinking. At length, the most glib recitation becomes the best; and the less the scholars are delayed by thought, the faster they can prate, as a mill clacks quicker when there is no grist in the hopper. Thoroughness, therefore, — thoroughness, and again I say, *thoroughness,* for the sake of the knowledge, and still more for the sake of the habit, — should, at all events, be enforced; and a pupil should never be suffered to leave any subject, until he can reach his arms quite around it, and clench his hands upon the opposite side. Those persons, who know a little of every thing but nothing well, have been aptly compared to a certain sort of pocket-knife, which some over-curious people carry about with them, which, in addition to a common knife, contains a file, a chisel, a saw, a gimlet, a screw-driver, and a pair of scissors, but all so diminutive, that the moment they are needed for use, they are found useless.

It seems to me that one of the greatest errors in education, at the present time, is the desire and ambition, at single lessons, to teach complex truths, whole systems, doctrines, theorems, which years of analysis are scarcely sufficient to unfold; instead of commencing with simple elements, and then rising, by gradations, to combined results. All is administered in a mass. We strive to introduce knowledge into the child's mind, the great end first. When lessons are given in this way, the pupil, being unable to comprehend the ideas, tries to remember the words, and thus, at best, is sent away with a single fact, instead of a principle, explanatory of whole classes of facts. The lessons are learned by rote; and when a teacher practises upon the rote system, he uses the minds of the pupils, just as they use their own slates, in working arithmetical questions; — whenever a second question is to be wrought, the first is sponged out, to make room for it. What would be thought of a teacher of music, who should give his pupils the most complicated exercises, before they had learned to sound simple notes? It is said of the athlete, Milo of Crotona, that he began by lifting a calf, and, continuing to lift it daily, he gained strength as fast as the animal gained weight; so that he was able to lift it, when it became an ox. Had he begun by straining to lift an ox, he would probably have broken down, and been afterwards unable to lift even a calf. The point to which I would invite the regards of the whole community, is, whether greater attention should not be paid to gradation, to progression in a natural order, to adjustment, to the preparation of a child's mind for receiving the higher forms of truth, by first making it thoroughly acquainted with their elements. The temptation to this error is perhaps the most seductive, that ever beguiles a teacher from his duty. He desires to make his pupils *appear* well. He forgets that the great objects of their education lie in the power, and dignity, and virtue of life, and not in their recitations, at the end of the quarter. Hence he strives to prepare them for the hastening day of exhibition. They must be able to state, in words, the great results, in science, which human reason has achieved, after almost sixty centuries of labor. For this purpose, — in which they also are tempted to conspire, — he loads their memories with burden after burden of definitions and formulas; which is about as useful a process, — and is it not also about as honest? — as it would be for the rearer of nursery trees to buy golden pippins in the market, and, tying them upon the branches of his young trees, to palm them off upon purchasers, as though the delicious fruit had been elaborated from the succulence of the stock he sells.

Another question of method, to which I most earnestly solicit the attention of teachers and of the whole public, is, whether there is not too much teaching of words, instead of things. Never was a severer satire uttered against human reason, than that of Mirabeau, when he said, "words are things." That single phrase explains the whole French Revolution. Such a revolution never could have occurred amongst a people who spoke things, instead of words. Just so far as words are things, just so far the infinite contexture of realities pertaining to body and soul, to earth and heaven, to time and eternity, is nothing. The ashes, and shreds, and wrecks of every thing else are of some value; but of words not freighted with ideas, there is no salvage. It is not *words,* but words *fitly spoken,* that are like apples of gold in pictures of silver. Words are but purses; things, the shining coin within them. Why buy seventy or eighty thousand purses, — for it is said we have about that number of untechnical words in the language, — without a copper for deposit? I believe it is almost universally true, that young students desire to be composers; and as universally true, that they dread composition. When they would compose, of what service, then, are those columns of spelling-book words, which they have committed to memory by the furlong? Where then, too, are the rich mines of thought contained in their Readers, their First-Class Books, and their little libraries? These they have been accustomed to consider merely as instruments, to practise pronunciation, emphasis, and cadence, upon. They have moved, for years, in the midst of ideas, like blind men in picture-galleries. Hence they have no knowledge of things and their relations; and, when called upon for composition, they have nothing to compound. But, as the outward and visible sign of composition is a sheet-full of words, a sheet is filled, though more from the dictionary than from the head. This practice comes at last, to make them a kind of sportsmen or warriors, who think their whole business is to fire, not to hit. Some, who have a strong verbal memory, become dexterous in the use of language; so that, if they can have two ideas, on any subject, to set up at the ends, as termini, they will fill up with words any distance of space between them. Those who have not this verbal memory, become the wind-driven bubbles of those who have. When the habit is confirmed, of relying on the verbal faculty, the rest of the mind dies out. The dogma taught by Aristotle, that Nature abhors a vacuum, is experimentally refuted. I know of but one compensation for these word-men; I believe they never become insane. Insanity requires some mind, for a basis.

The subject of penal discipline, I hardly dare to mention; especially discipline by corporal punishment. In this department, extremes both of doctrine and of practice prevail. The, public have taken sides, and parties are arrayed against each other. Some repudiate and .condemn it, altogether. With others, it is the great motive-power; and they consider it as, at least, the first and second, if not the three estates in the realm of school-keeping. Generally speaking, I fear that but little judgment and forethought are brought to the decision of its momentous questions. It cannot be discussed, alone. It is closely connected with intellectual progress; its influences pervade the whole moral nature; and it must be looked at, in its relations to them. The justifiable occasions, if any, for inflicting it; the mode, and emphatically, the spirit, of its administration; its instruments; its extent; the conduct that should precede and should follow it, — are questions worthy of the deepest attention. That corporal punishment, considered by itself, and without reference to its ultimate object, is an evil, probably none will deny. Yet, with almost three thousand public schools in this State, composed of all kinds of children, with about six thousand teachers, of all grades of qualification, to govern them, probably the evils of corporal punishment must be endured, or the greater ones of insubordination and mutiny be incurred. I hesitate also to speak so fully of the magnitude of these evils, as I would wish to do; because there are some excellent teachers, who manage schools without resorting to it; while others, ambitious for the same honor, but destitute of skill and of the divine qualities of love, patience, sympathy, by which alone it can be won,' have discarded what they call corporal punishment, but have resorted to other modes of discipline, which, though they may bear a milder name, are, in reality, more severe. To imprison timid children in a dark and solitary place; to brace open the jaws with a piece of wood; to torture the muscles and bones, by the strain of an unnatural position, or of holding an enormous weight; to inflict a wound upon the instinctive feelings of modesty and delicacy, by making a girl sit with the boys, or go out with them, at recess; to bring a whole class around a fellow-pupil, to ridicule and shame him; to break down the spirit of self-respect, by enforcing some ignominious compliance; to give a nick-name; — these, and such as these, are the gentle appliances, by which some teachers, who profess to discard corporal punishment, maintain the empire of the schoolroom; — as though the muscles and bones were less corporeal than the skin; as though a wound of the spirit were of less moment than one of the flesh; and the body's blood more sacred than the soul's purity. But of these solemn topics, it is impossible here to speak. I cannot, however, forbear to express the opinion, that punishment should never be inflicted, except in cases of the extremest necessity; while the experiment of sympathy, confidence, persuasion, encouragement, should be repeated, for ever and ever. The fear of bodily pain is a degrading motive; but we have authority for saying, that where there is perfect love, every known law will be fulfilled. Parents and teachers often create that disgust at study, and that incorrigibleness and obstinacy of disposition, which they deplore. It is a sad exchange, if the very blows, which beat arithmetic and grammar into a boy, should beat confidence and manliness out. So it is quite as important to consider what feelings are excited, in the mind, as what are subdued, by the punishment. Which side gains, though the evil spirit of roguery or wantonness be driven out, if seven other evil spirits, worse than the first, — sullenness, irreverence, fraud, lying, hatred, malice, revenge, — are allowed to come in? The motive from which the offence emanated, and the motives with which the culprit leaves the bar of his judge and executioner, are every thing. If these are not regarded, the offender may go away worse than he came, in addition to a gratuitous flagellation. To say a child knows better, is nothing; if he knows better, why does he not do better? The answer to this question reveals the difficulty; and whoever has not patience and sagacity to solve that inquiry, Is as unworthy of the parental trust, as is the physician, of administering to the sick, who prescribes a fatal nostrum, and says, in justification, that he knew nothing of the disease. In fine, if any thing, in the wide range of education, demands patience, forethought, judgment, and the all-subduing spirit of love, it is this; and though it may be too much to say, that corporal punishment can be disused by all teachers, with regard to all scholars, in all schools, yet it may be averred, without exception, that it is never inflicted with the right spirit, nor in the right measure, when it is not more painful to him who imposes, than to him who receives it.

Of emulation in school, as an incitement to effort, I can here say but a word; but I entreat all intelligent men to give to this subject a most careful consideration. And let those who use it, as a quickener of the intellect, beware, lest it prove a depraver of the social affections. There is no necessary incompatibility between the upward progress of one portion of our nature, and the lower and lower debasement of another. The intellect may grow wise, while the passions grow wicked. No cruelty towards a child can be so great as that which barters morals for attainment. If, under the fiery stimulus of emulation, the pupil comes to regard a successful rival with envy or malevolence, or an unsuccessful one with arrogance or disdain; if, in aiming at the goal of precedence, he loses sight of the goal of perfection; if, to gain his prize, he becomes the hypocrite, instead of the reverer of virtue; — then, though his intellect should enter upon the stage of life with all the honors of an early triumph; yet the noblest parts of his nature, — his moral and social affections, — will be the victims, led captive in the retinue. Suppose, in some Theological Seminary, a prize were offered for the best exposition of the commandment, *"Thou shall love thy neighbor as thyself,"* and two known competitors were to task their intellects, to win it; — and, on the day of trial, one of these neighbor-loving rivals, with dilated nostril and expanded frame, should clutch the honor; while the other neighbor-loving rival, with quivering lip and livid countenance, stood by, — the vulture of envy, all the while, forking her talons into his heart; — would it not be that very mixture of the ludicrous and the horrible, which demons would choose for the subject of an epigram! Paint, or chisel the whole group of neighbor-loving rivals, and pious doctors sitting around and mingling, — in one chalice, the hellebore of pride, and in another, the wormwood of defeat, — to be administered to those who should be brothers, and can aught be found more worthy to fill a niche in the council-hall of Pandemonium! Who has not seen winter, with its deepest congelations, come in between ingenuous-minded and loving fellow-students, whose hearts would otherwise have run together, like kindred drops of water? Who has not witnessed a consumption, — not of the lungs, but of the heart; nay, both of lungs and heart, — wasting its victims with the smothered frenzy of emulation? It surely is within the equity of the prayer, "lead *us* not into temptation," not to lead others into it. And ought not the teacher, who, as a general and prevalent, — I do not say a universal rule,— cannot sustain order and insure proficiency, in a school, without resorting to fear and emulation, to consider, whether the fault be in human nature or in himself? And will there ever be any more of that secret, silent beneficence amongst us, where the left hand knows not of the blessings scattered by the right? — will there ever be any less of this deadly strife for the ostensible signs of precedence, in the social and political arena, while the germs of emulation are so assiduously cultivated in the schoolroom, the academy, and the college? The pale ambition of men, ready to sacrifice country and kind for self, is only the fire of youthful emulation, heated to a white heat. Yet, there is an inborn sentiment of emulation, in all minds, and there are external related objects of that sentiment. The excellent, who may be present with us, but who are advanced in life; the great and good, who are absent, but whose fame is every where; the illustrious dead; — these are the objects of emulation. A rivalry with these yields sacred love, not consuming envy. On these, therefore, let the emulous and aspiring gaze, until their eyes overflow with tears, and every tear will be the baptism of honor and of purity.

Such are some of the most obvious topics, belonging to that sacred work, — the education of children. The science, or philosophical principles on which this work is to be conducted; the art, or manner in which those principles are to be applied, must all be rightly settled and generally understood, before any system of Public Instruction can operate with efficiency. Yet all this has been mainly left to chance. Compared with its deserts, how disproportionate, how little, the labor, cost and talent, devoted to it. We have a Congress, convening annually, at almost incredible expense, to decide upon questions of tariff, internal improvement, and currency. We have a State Legislature, continuing in session more than a fourth part of every year, to regulate our internal polity. We have Courts, making continual circuits through the Commonwealth to adjudicate upon doubtful rights of person or property, however trivial. Every great department of literature and of business has its Periodical. Every party, political, religious and social, has its Press. Yet Education, that vast cause, of which all other causes are only constituent parts; that cause, on which all other causes are dependent, for their vitality and usefulness, — if I except the American Institute of Instruction, and a few local, feeble, unpatronized, though worthy associations, — Education has literally nothing, in the way of comprehensive organization and of united effort, acting for a common end and under the focal light of a common intelligence. It is under these circumstances; it is in view of these great public wants, that the Board of Education has been established, — not to legislate, not to enforce, — but to collect facts, to educe principles, to diffuse a knowledge of improvements; — in fine, to submit the views of men who have thought much upon this subject to men who have thought but little.

To specify the labors which education has yet to perform, would be only to pass in review the varied interests of humanity. Its general purposes are to preserve the good and to repudiate the evil which now exist, and to give scope to the sublime law of progression. It is its duty to take the accumulations in knowledge, of almost six thousand years, and to transfer the vast treasure to posterity. Suspend its functions for but one generation, and the experience and the achievements of the past are lost. The race must commence its fortunes anew, and must again spend six thousand years, before it can grope its way upward from barbarism to the present point of civilization. With the wisdom, education must also teach something of the follies, of the past, for admonition and warning; for it has been well said, that mankind have seldom arrived at truth, on any subject, until they had first exhausted its errors.

Education is to instruct the whole people in the proper care of the body, in order to augment the powers of that wonderful machine, and to prevent so much of disease, of suffering, and of premature death. The body is the mind's instrument; and the powers of the mind, like the skill of an artisan, may all be baffled, through the imperfection of their utensils. The happiness and the usefulness of thousands and tens of thousands of men and women have been destroyed, from not knowing a few of the simple laws of health, which they might have learned in a few months; — nay, which might have been so impressed upon them, as habits, in childhood, that they would never think there was any other way. I do not speak of the ruin, that comes from slavery to throned appetites, where the bondage might continue in defiance of knowledge; but I speak of cases, where the prostration of noble powers and the suffering of terrible maladies result from sheer ignorance and false views of the wise laws to which God has subjected our physical nature. No doubt, Voltaire said truly, that the fate of many a nation had depended upon the good or bad digestion of its minister; and how much more extensively true would the remark be, if applied to individuals? How many men perfectly understand the observances by which their horses and cattle are made healthy and strong; while their children are puny, distempered, and have chronic diseases, at the very earliest age, at which so highly-finished an article as a chronic disease can be prepared. There is a higher art than the art of the physician; — the art, not of *restoring,* but of *making* health. Health is a product. Health is a manufactured article, — as much so as any fabric of the loom or the workshop; and, except in some few cases of hereditary taint or of organic lesion from accident or violence, the how much, or the how little, health any man shall enjoy, depends upon his treatment of himself; or rather, upon the treatment of those who manage his infancy and childhood, and create his habits for him. Situated, as we are, in a high latitude, with the Atlantic ocean on one side and a range of mountains on the other, we cannot escape frequent and great transitions, in the temperature of our weather. Our region is the perpetual battle-ground of the torrid and the arctic, where they alternately prevail; and it is only by a sort of average that we call it *temperate*. Yet to this natural position we must adapt ourselves, or abandon it, or suffer. Hence the necessity of making health, in order to endure natural inclemencies; and hence the necessity of including the simple and benign laws on which it depends, in all our plans of education. Certainly, our hearts should glow with gratitude to Heaven, for all the means of health; but every expression indicating that health is a Divine gift, in any other sense than all our blessings are a Divine gift, should be discarded from the language; and it should be incorporated into the forms of speech, that a man prepares his own health, as he does his own house.

Education is to inspire the love of truth, as the supremest good, and to clarify the vision of the intellect to discern it. We want a generation of men above deciding great and eternal principles, upon narrow and selfish grounds. Our advanced state of civilization has evolved many complicated questions respecting social duties. We want a generation of men capable of taking up these complex questions, and of turning all sides of them towards the sun, and of examining them by the white light of reason, and not under the false colors which sophistry may throw upon them. We want no men who will change, like the vanes of our steeples, with the course of the popular wind; but we want men who, like mountains, will change the course of the wind. We want no more of those patriots who exhaust their patriotism, in lauding the past; but we want patriots who will do for the future what the past has done for us. We want men capable of deciding, not merely what is right, in principle, — *that* is often the smallest part of the case;— but we want men capable of deciding what is right in means, to accomplish what is right in principle. We want men who will speak to this great people in counsel, and not in flattery. We want god-like men who can tame the madness of the times, and, speaking divine words in a divine spirit, can say to the raging of human passions, "Peace, be still;" and usher in the calm of enlightened reason and conscience. Look at our community, divided into so many parties and factions, and these again subdivided, on all questions of social, national, and international, duty; — while, over all, stands, almost unheeded, the sublime form of Truth, eternally and indissolubly *One!* Nay, further, those do not agree in thought who agree in words. Their unanimity is a delusion. It arises from the imperfection of language. Could men, who subscribe to the same forms of words, but look into each other's minds, and see, there, what features their own idolized doctrines wear, friends would often start back from the friends they have loved, with as much abhorrence as from the enemies they have persecuted. Now, what can save us from endless contention, but the love of truth? What can save us, and our children after us, from eternal, implacable, universal war, but the greatest of all human powers, — the power of impartial thought? Many, — may I not say most, — of those great questions, which make the present age boil and seethe, like a cauldron, will never be settled, until we have a generation of men who were educated, from childhood, to seek for truth and to revere justice. In the middle of the last century, a great dispute arose among astronomers, respecting one of the planets. Some, in their folly, commenced a war of words, and wrote hot books against each other; others, in their wisdom, improved their telescopes, and soon settled the question forever. Education should imitate the latter. If there are momentous questions which, with present lights, we cannot demonstrate and determine, let us rear up stronger, and purer, and more impartial, minds, for the solemn arbitrament. Let it be for ever and ever inculcated, that no bodily wounds or maim, no deformity of person, nor disease of brain, or lungs, or heart, can be so disabling or so painful, as error; and that he who heals us of our prejudices is a thousand fold more our benefactor, than he who heals us of mortal maladies. Teach children, if you will, to beware of the bite of a mad dog; but teach them still more faithfully, that no horror of water is so fatal as a horror of truth, because it does not come from our leader or our party. Then shall we have more men who will think, as it were, under oath; — not thousandth and ten thousandth transmitters of falsity; — not copyists of copyists, and blind followers of blind followers; but men who can track the Deity in his ways of wisdom. A love of truth, — *a love of truth;* this is the pool of a moral Bethesda, whose waters have miraculous healing. And though we lament that we cannot bequeath to posterity this precious boon, in its perfectness, as the greatest of all patrimonies, yet let us rejoice that we can inspire a love of it, a reverence for it, a devotion to it; and thus circumscribe and weaken whatever is wrong, and enlarge and strengthen whatever is right, in that mixed inheritance of good and evil, which, in the order of Providence, one generation transmits to another.

If we contemplate the subject with the eye of a statesman, what resources are there, in the whole domain of Nature, at all comparable to that vast influx of power which comes into the world with every incoming generation of children? Each embryo life is more wonderful than the globe it is sent to inhabit, and more glorious than the sun upon which it first opens its eyes. Each one of these millions, with a fitting education, is capable of adding something to the sum of human happiness, and of subtracting something from the sum of human misery; and many great souls amongst them there are, who may become instruments for turning the course of nations, as the rivers of water are turned. It is the duty of moral and religious education to employ and administer all these capacities of good, for lofty purposes of human beneficence, — as a wise minister employs the resources of a great empire. "Suffer little children to come unto me," said the Savior, "and forbid them not, for of such is the kingdom of Heaven." And who shall dare say, that philanthropy and religion cannot make a better world than the present, from beings like those in the kingdom of Heaven!

Education must be universal. It is well, when the wise and the learned discover new truths; but how much better to diffuse the truths already discovered, amongst the multitude! Every addition to true knowledge is an addition to human power; and while a philosopher is discovering one new truth, millions may be propagated amongst the people. Diffusion, then, rather than discovery, is the duty of .our government. With us, the qualification of voters is as important as the qualification of governors, and even comes first, in the natural order. Yet there is no Sabbath of rest, in our contests about the latter, while so little is done to qualify the former. The theory of our government is, — not that all men, however unfit, shall be voters, — but that every man, by the power of reason and the sense of duty, shall become fit to be a voter. Education must bring the practice as nearly as possible to the theory. As the children now are, so will the sovereigns soon be. How can we expect the fabric of the government to stand, if vicious materials are daily wrought into its framework? Education must prepare our citizens to become municipal officers, intelligent jurors, honest witnesses, legislators, or competent judges of legislation, — in fine, to fill all the manifold relations of life. For this end, it must be universal. The whole land must be watered with the streams of knowledge. It is not enough to have, here and there, a beautiful fountain playing in palace-gardens; but let it come like the abundant fatness of the clouds upon the thirsting earth.

Finally, education, alone, can conduct us to that enjoyment which is, at once, best in quality and infinite in quantity. God has revealed to us, — not by ambiguous signs, but by His mighty works; — not in the disputable language of human invention, but by the solid substance and reality of things, — what He holds to be valuable, and what He regards as of little account. The latter He has created sparingly, as though it were nothing worth; while the former He has poured forth with immeasurable munificence. I suppose all the diamonds ever found, could be hid under a bushel. Their quantity is little, because their value is small. But iron ore, — without which mankind would always have been barbarians; without which they would now relapse into barbarism, — he has strewed profusely all over the earth. Compare the scantiness of pearl, with the extent of forests and coal-fields. Of one, little has been created, because it is worth little; of the others, much, because they are worth much. His fountains of naphtha, how few, and myrrh and frankincense, how exiguous; but who can fathom His reservoirs of water, or measure the light and the air! This principle pervades every realm of Nature. Creation seems to have been projected upon the plan of increasing the quantity, in the ratio of the intrinsic value. Emphatically is this plan manifested, when we come to that part of creation we call *our-*

selves. Enough of the materials of worldly good has been created to answer this great principle,— that, up to the point of competence, up to the point of independence and self-respect, few things are more valuable than property; beyond that point, few things are of less. And hence it is, that all acquisitions of property, beyond that point, — considered and used as mere property, — confer an inferior sort of pleasure, in inferior quantities. However rich a man may be, a certain number of thicknesses of woollens or of silks is all he can comfortably wear. Give him a dozen palaces, he can live in but one at a lime. Though the commander be worth the whole regiment, or ship's company, he can have the animal pleasure of eating only his own rations j and any other animal eats, with as much relish as he. Hence the wealthiest, with all their wealth, are driven back to a cultivated mind, to beneficent uses and appropriations; and it is then, and then only, that a glorious vista of happiness opens out into immensity and immortality.

Education, then, is to show to our youth, in early life, this broad line of demarcation between the value of those things which can be owned and enjoyed by but one, and those which can be owned and enjoyed by all. If I own a ship, a house, a farm, or a mass of the metals called precious, my right to them is, in its nature, sole and exclusive. No other man has a right to trade with my ship, to occupy my house, to gather my harvests, or to appropriate my treasures to his use. They are mine, and are incapable, both of a sole and of a joint possession. But not so of the treasures of knowledge, which it is the duty of education to diffuse. The same truth may enrich and ennoble all intelligences at once. Infinite diffusion subtracts nothing from depth. None are made poor because others are made rich. In this part of the Divine economy, the privilege of primogeniture attaches to all; and every son and daughter of Adam are heirs to an infinite patrimony. If I own an exquisite picture or statue, it is mine, exclusively. Even though publicly exhibited, but few could be charmed by its beauties, at the same time. It is incapable of bestowing a pleasure, simultaneous and universal. But not so of the beauty of a moral sentiment; not so of the glow of sublime emotion; not so of the feelings of conscious purity and rectitude. These may shed rapture upon all, without deprivation of any; be imparted, and still possessed; transferred to millions, yet never surrendered; carried out of the world, and still left in it. These may imparadise mankind, and, undiluted, unattenuated, be sent round the whole orb of being. Let education, then, teach children this great truth, written as it is on the fore-front of the universe, that God has so constituted this world, into which He has sent them, that whatever is really and truly valuable may be possessed by all, and possessed in exhaustless abundance.

And now, you, my friends! who feel that you are patriots and lovers of mankind, — what bulwarks, what ramparts for freedom can you devise, so enduring and impregnable, as intelligence and virtue! Parents! among the happy groups of children whom you have at home, —

more dear to you than the blood in the fountain of life, — you have not a son nor a daughter who, in this world of temptation, is not destined to encounter perils more dangerous than to walk a bridge of a single plank, over a dark and sweeping torrent, beneath. But it is in your power and at your option, with the means which Providence will graciously vouchsafe, to give them that firmness of intellectual movement and that keenness of moral vision, — that light of knowledge and that omnipotence of virtue, — by which, in the hour of trial, they will be able to walk, with unfaltering step, over the deep and yawning abyss, below, and to reach the opposite shore, in safety, and honor, and happiness.

www.ingramcontent.com/pod-product-compliance
Lightning Source LLC
Chambersburg PA
CBHW031333040426
42443CB00005B/322

* 9 7 8 1 7 8 9 8 7 5 6 1 4 *